THE
BIBLE
Storybook

THE
BIBLE

Storybook

Georgie Adams *Illustrated by* Peter Utton

Orion
Children's Books

For Judith Elliott who inspired this book,

with grateful thanks and appreciation for her

invaluable editorial guidance—G.A.

To Harry—P.U.

First published in Great Britain in 1994
Reprinted in 1995
by Orion Children's Books
a division of the Orion Publishing Group Ltd
Orion House
5 Upper St Martin's Lane
London WC2H 9EA

Text copyright © Georgie Adams 1994
Illustrations copyright © Peter Utton 1994
Designed by Ian Butterworth

A catalogue record for this book is available from the British Library

Printed in Italy
ISBN 1 85881 042 6

Contents

Foreword

When I sat down to write this book, I imagined how I would have told these stories to my children – adding my own thoughts here and there, with a good measure of humour too. Storytelling was a special time we shared together. With this in mind I wrote these stories to be told, in the way people passed them on to each other thousands of years ago, long before they were written down, which is how the Bible began.

The Bible is like a library – the word 'Bible' means books. There are sixty-six smaller books in the one big book called the Bible. It would take ages to read it all at once! There are two main parts – the Old Testament and the New Testament.

The Old Testament was written before Jesus was born. The stories in this part are about God and His chosen people, the Israelites. That's where you'll find exciting stories about Noah, Joseph and David, among others, who loved God and tried to be good. The

New Testament tells us about the life of Jesus, the Son of God. In this part there are stories about Jesus performing miracles and healing the sick – each one full of mystery and meaning.

In time, these events were written about in tales, songs and legends. It took hundreds of years to collect all those early writings to make the Bible. So you see, it has been around for a very long time.

But the language of the Bible is not always easy to understand. So I have chosen some of the best-loved stories and retold them. I imagined how things might have been (the Bible doesn't always say), and introduced my own ideas where I think they help to bring characters and events to life – careful always to preserve the spirit and message of these wonderful stories.

I hope you'll enjoy *The Bible Storybook* at bedtime or anytime – over and over again!

Georgie Adams

Noah's Ark

There was once a man called Noah, who loved God and tried to be good. Noah had a wife and three sons called Shem, Ham, and Japheth. Noah, his wife, the sons and their wives all worked hard.

God was pleased with Noah and his family, but he wasn't too happy about everyone else. He looked around and saw people fighting, stealing, and telling lies. No wonder he wasn't pleased.

I'm sorry I made people, thought God. I'll destroy everything and begin again. But it didn't seem fair that Noah's family should be punished too, so God thought of a plan to save them.

"I'm going to send a flood that will drown all the wicked people and the whole earth," God told Noah one day. "But if you do as I say, you and your family will be safe."

God told Noah to build an ark. He gave him the exact measurements for the boat. It would have three decks, a window, and a door. Noah wrote the plans down carefully. The ark was going to be enormous! God explained why:

"Many animals will be lost in the flood," he said. "I want you to take a male and female of every kind on board with you. Look after them until the flood goes down. Then let them go to make new homes for their young. Remember to pack enough food for everyone."

Noah started work on the ark immediately. Shem, Ham, and

Japheth cut down trees, and sawed and sliced them into planks. They needed a lot of wood.

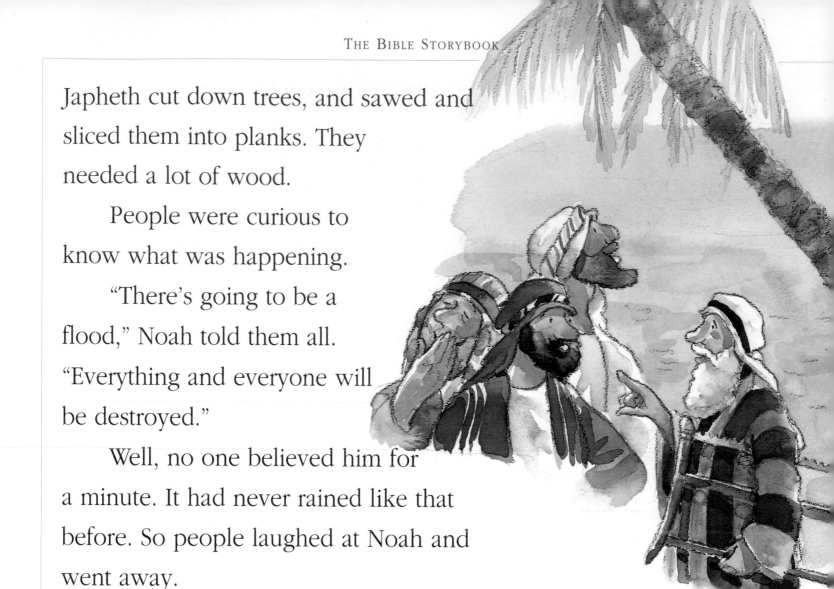

People were curious to know what was happening.

"There's going to be a flood," Noah told them all. "Everything and everyone will be destroyed."

Well, no one believed him for a minute. It had never rained like that before. So people laughed at Noah and went away.

While Noah was busy building the ark, his sons went to look for the animals. They rounded them up and brought them back in pairs. The animals came roaring, bleating, grunting, and squawking. What a noise!

The women made a list of things they would need:

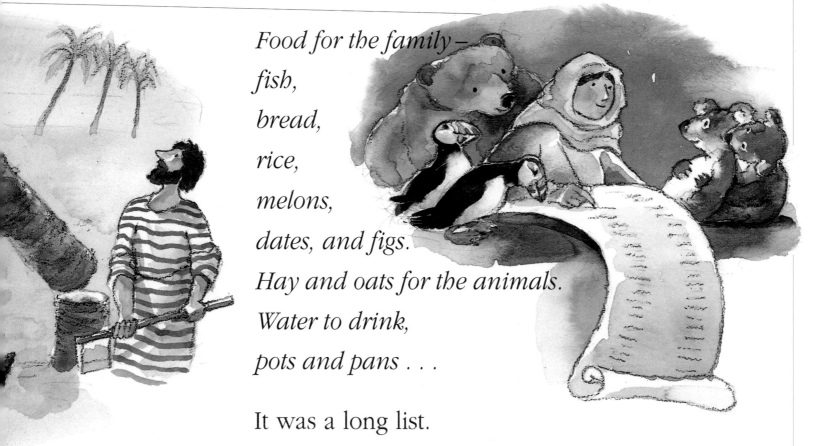

Food for the family —
fish,
bread,
rice,
melons,
dates, and figs.
Hay and oats for the animals.
Water to drink,
pots and pans . . .

It was a long list.

Meanwhile Noah and his sons were putting the finishing touches to the ark. They painted it with sticky tar to keep the water out. And when that was done, the ark was ready.

God told Noah that the flood would start in a week. It would rain for forty days and forty nights.

So Noah said to Shem, Ham, and Japheth, "Start loading up!"

After seven days everything was on board. As Noah watched the last two animals trot inside, he felt the first drop of rain on his head. Then he took his family into the ark and shut the door.

It poured. Rain fell from the sky like a sheet of water. Rivers overflowed. Fields became lakes. Lakes turned into seas.

The ark creaked and rolled, but it stayed afloat. The flood rose higher and higher. Over the trees. Over the hills. Over the mountains! Noah listened to the rain hammering on the roof. He could hear the waves slapping against the hull. And still it kept raining.

One morning about six weeks later, Noah woke up and listened. He couldn't hear a thing. The rain had stopped. He looked out of the window.

The sun was shining. There wasn't a cloud in sight.

It took ages for the floodwaters to go down. The ark drifted for weeks, until one day *bump!* it ran aground.

Noah opened the window and looked over the side. They seemed to be stuck on a mountain.

Everyone wanted to get out and stretch their legs, but the ark was still surrounded by water.

Noah brought a dove to the window and let it fly out. He wanted to see if the bird could find dry land. But the dove came back before sunset, tired and hungry. It had found nothing.

A week later Noah sent the dove out again. This time it came back with an olive twig. It had found a tree to perch on.

Seven days after that, Noah sent the dove off a third time. But this time it didn't return, so he knew it had found land.

Noah opened the door. There were a few puddles, but that was all.

"Look!" cried Noah. "The flood is gone."

It was wonderful to be outside again. The world looked fresh and green after all that rain.

Noah and his family helped the animals out of the ark. They came clattering down the ramp two by two. A male and female of every kind. Every creature free to make a new start.

God promised Noah that he would never send another flood to destroy the world. And when God makes a promise, he keeps it.

"I'll give you a sign," said God. "Whenever it's cloudy and a rainbow appears in the sky, you will know that I have remembered my promise to you, your family, and all the animals. No more floods!"

God kept his word and Noah told everyone about the rainbow.

The next time you see a rainbow, perhaps you'll tell someone about Noah and the flood and God's promise, too?

Joseph

and his Coat of Many Colours

There was a boy called Joseph who had eleven brothers. It was a job keeping everyone happy in that family, I can tell you. Once, Joseph told his father that his older brothers were not looking after the flocks properly. It made them angry with Joseph.

Jacob, the boys' father, loved Joseph more than all the rest, which wasn't fair, but that's how it was. One day he gave his favourite son a fine coat of many colours. There wasn't another one like it for miles around. And Joseph wore it everywhere.

All this made his brothers very jealous.

"Look at us," said Judah. "Here we are minding the animals and cutting corn. And what's Joseph doing? Wandering around in that new coat, daydreaming!"

It was true. Joseph was a dreamer. At night he had strange dreams that he could remember clearly the next day.

"Listen to this," Joseph said to his brothers one morning. "In my dream we were bundling corn into sheaves. Suddenly my sheaf stood up straight and your sheaves bowed down to it."

Joseph's brothers didn't like the sound of that.

"How dare you suggest that we should bow to you!" said Daniel.

It was only a dream, but that's what it meant. It made the brothers even angrier.

A few days later Joseph had another dream. This time he told the whole family about it.

"In my dream I saw the sun, the moon, and eleven stars all bow down to me," said Joseph.

Well, that did it. Even his father was angry. The sun and moon sounded very much like Jacob and his wife. You can guess who the eleven stars were!

Although he was upset, Jacob thought a lot about this dream. Could it be a sign from God that Joseph was to be the most special person in the family?

The farm where Joseph lived had only a few scrubby bushes for the sheep and goats to eat. So one day the brothers – all except Joseph and little Benjamin – packed some food and took the animals to better land.

After a while Jacob began to worry. He asked Joseph to go and look for them.

"Make sure they are safe," said Jacob, as he waved good-bye to his favourite son.

It took Joseph a long time to find his brothers. Up one hill and down another. It was exhausting. And, of course, he insisted on wearing that coat! But at last he saw them.

Perhaps the sight of that coat brought all the feelings of jealousy back to them, because at that moment his brothers began to plot against him.

"Let's kill him," said one.

"No," said Reuben. "We'll just put him down that dried-up well for a while. That'll teach him a lesson!"

So they grabbed Joseph and dragged him to the well.

"Let me go!" shouted Joseph, kicking and struggling to get free. "Mind my coat, you'll tear it!"

Joseph's brothers did mind his coat. They took it right off, then threw Joseph into the well. It was a deep pit. There was no escape. After that, as if nothing had happened, they sat down and had lunch. All except Reuben, who had gone to look for a stray lamb.

They had just finished eating, when along came some merchants on their way to Egypt. Judah had an idea. It wasn't a very nice one.

"Let's sell Joseph to the merchants," he said.

In those days people could be bought and sold in a slave market. The brothers could get rid of Joseph and earn some money too.

So while Reuben was still away, the others lifted Joseph out of the pit and sold him. They were paid twenty silver pieces, which was a good price.

By the time Reuben got back, Joseph had gone. At first Reuben thought the others had killed him. Then Daniel told him what they had done. Reuben was horrified to hear that Joseph had been taken to Egypt as a slave. But it was too late to do anything about it. What *would* they tell Jacob?

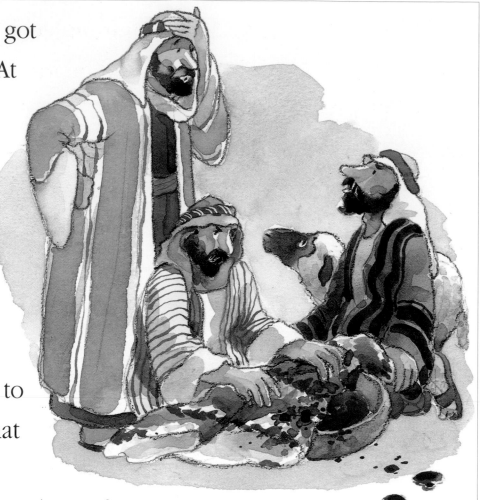

Judah, who was never short of nasty ideas, had a plan.

"We'll put some goat's blood on Joseph's coat," he said. "Father will think he was killed by a wild animal."

It was a cruel thing to do, but Jacob was sure to believe it. When the brothers returned home, you can imagine how upset Jacob was to see the bloodstained coat: Joseph's coat of many colours.

Tears fell from Jacob's eyes. The old man said he would be sad for the rest of his life.

Little did Jacob know that he *would* see his son again. For Joseph, the dreamer, became one of the most important people in Egypt. It happened like this:

During his time as a slave, Joseph was put into prison for something he hadn't done. While he was there, he told the other prisoners the meaning of their dreams. And he was always right!

Word soon got around, and one day the king of Egypt heard about Joseph. He asked him to explain the meaning of some strange dreams he was having.

The king was so pleased with Joseph that he set him free and made him governor of Egypt. Joseph did his job well, and made sure there was always enough food for people to eat.

Many years later Joseph's brothers came to Egypt to buy corn.
The crops in their own country had dried up. Their families at home
were starving. They had to go down on their knees and beg the
governor of Egypt for food! So you see, Joseph's dream about his
brothers bowing down before him came true.

At first the brothers did not recognise Joseph. But then he told them who he was. Joseph forgave his brothers for treating him so badly all those years ago. He sent them home with sacks full of corn, food, and money.

When the brothers returned home, Jacob could hardly believe the news about Joseph. His favourite son was alive!

So Jacob took his family to Egypt and saw Joseph again, and they all lived there happily for many years.

Moses

in the Bulrushes

The king of Egypt was worried. People from Israel had been living in his country for many years and having lots of children. If things went on like this, soon there would be more of them than Egyptians. Something had to be done.

So the king made a new law. Every Israelite baby boy was to be drowned in the River Nile. It was a terrible law, but the Israelites had to obey.

One day a baby boy was born to a mother called Jochebed. She and her husband already had a fine son and a daughter, called Miriam.

Jochebed loved her new baby and couldn't bear to see him taken away.

For three whole months she kept him hidden. It was difficult. Babies grow and babies cry. There came a day when Jochebed had to think of a better way to hide him from the Egyptian soldiers.

Jochebed had often stood on the banks of the River Nile and watched the fishermen in their reed boats. The boats were woven from the tough bulrushes that grew by the river. It gave her an idea.

Jochebed took a basket made of reeds and covered it with tar to make it watertight. Miriam watched her mother as she worked. The basket made a perfect floating cradle just big enough to hold her baby brother!

Miriam helped her mother wrap the baby to keep him warm. She cried as Jochebed gently laid him in the basket. Miriam loved her brother.

"It's for the best," said Jochebed, trying to comfort her. "We will hide him in the bulrushes. He will be safe there and you can keep watch over him."

Later, when they were sure no one was around, Miriam and her mother took the basket and hid it among the bulrushes. Then Jochebed went home, leaving Miriam to see what would happen.

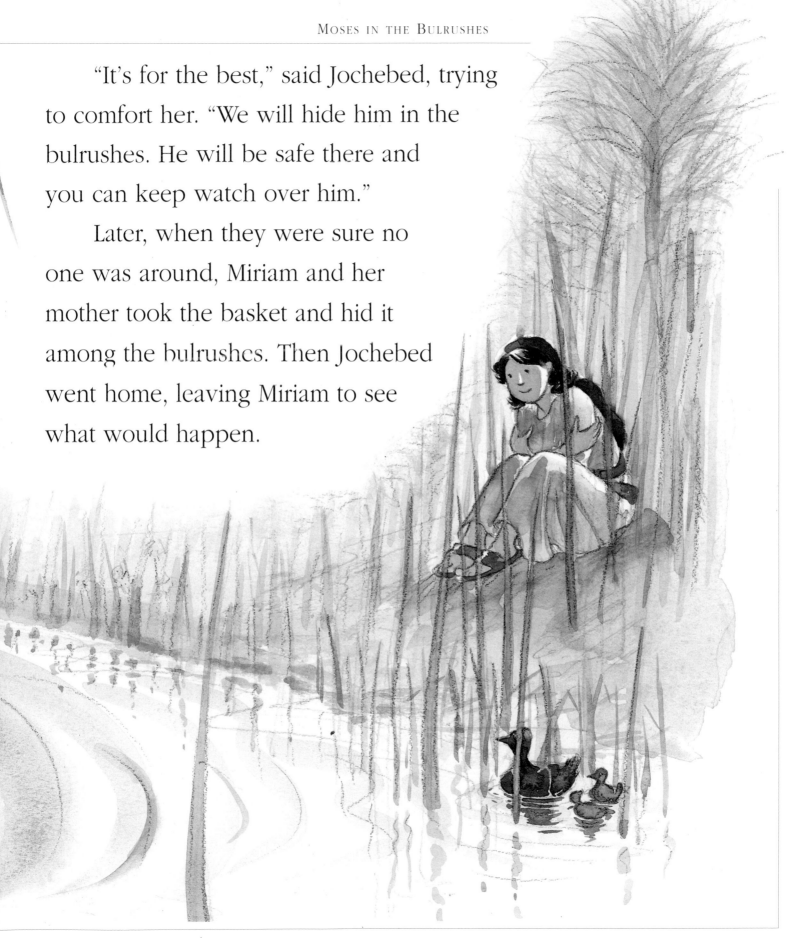

Miriam was standing just near enough to the bulrushes to see the baby's cradle. Suddenly she heard a voice cry out. The king's daughter had come down to the river to bathe. She had found the baby!

"What's that basket over there?" said the princess to one of her maids. "Bring it to me."

The maid waded into the water and lifted the cradle out of the bulrushes. The baby was sound asleep, but as the princess took him into her arms, he woke up and began to cry. She loved him at once.

"Poor thing, it must be one of the Israelite babies," said the princess.

At that moment Miriam stepped from her hiding place and spoke to the king's daughter.

"Would you like me to find an Israelite woman to feed and look after the baby for you?" she asked.

The princess was delighted. Miriam knew just the right person for the job. She ran all the way home and got her mother!

So Jochebed was able to care for her son after all. The princess paid Jochebed to nurse the baby until he was old enough to go and live with her in the palace. Then she adopted the boy as her own son and called him Moses.

Moses grew up to be a very wise man, and God chose him to lead his people out of Egypt to a country of their own.

David

and Goliath

A long time ago there was a boy called David. His job was to look after the sheep on his father's farm. He was very good at it.

Each day David took the flock up the mountain to graze. He had to watch it carefully because there were hungry lions and bears around. They were always on the lookout for a stray sheep. But young David wasn't afraid. Not at all. He was one of the bravest shepherds around.

Once, when a lion did manage to snatch a lamb, David ran after it. He was armed with just a small knife, a sling and a few stones. David put a stone in his sling. Then he whirled the sling around, took aim and let fly. The stone hit the lion *smack!* on the nose. It was so surprised that it dropped the lamb and ran, but David sprang at it and killed it with his knife. That's how brave he was!

When David wasn't busy with the sheep, he taught himself to play the harp. He was good at that too. One day King Saul heard about David and his music, and he asked the shepherd boy to play for him at the palace. So from that day on, David and the king got to know each other quite well.

Now King Saul and the people of Israel were having trouble with their old enemies, the Philistines. They were always quarrelling.

David's three oldest brothers were soldiers in King Saul's army. They had marched with the king to a mountain overlooking a valley. The Philistines were on the other side. The two armies stood facing each other, ready to do battle. Only this time things were different.

The Philistines had a soldier called Goliath, who was a real giant of a man. He was enormous! He wore a suit of heavy armour and had a shield as big as a door. To make matters worse, Goliath kept strutting up and down in front of King Saul's army, shouting at the top of his voice.

"Who's brave enough to fight me, eh?" bellowed Goliath. "Who's going to kill me?" he laughed. "Strike me dead, and we will be your slaves. But if I win . . . ha! Victory will be ours and you will be our slaves!"

He went on and on like that for weeks. It was terrifying. Nobody dared go near him.

At home David wondered how his brothers were getting on.

He would have loved to fight, but he had to stay at home and look after the flocks.

One evening his father said, "I want you to take some food to your brothers and see how they are."

So early next morning David set off for the mountain. It was a good long walk and when he got there, the battle was about to begin.

David found his brothers and they pointed to Goliath. "The king has promised that whoever kills Goliath will be rewarded with riches and shall marry his daughter," said one. "But there is no one brave enough to challenge him."

"Oh, yes, there is," said David. And he went straight to the king. "I'll fight Goliath for you."

At first the king refused. "You're just a boy," he said.

"I have killed a lion to save my father's sheep," said David. "God protected me then and he will save me from the giant."

The king wasn't too happy about it, but he agreed to let David try. He looked at David dressed in his thin tunic. "You must wear my armour," he said.

David tried it on, but everything was much too big. He couldn't move a step. So he took it all off, thanked the king, and said he would fight in his own way.

At a nearby stream, David chose five smooth, round stones and put them in a bag. Then he picked up his sling and went to meet Goliath.

The giant could hardly believe his eyes when he saw David. He had waited forty days for the king to choose somebody to fight him, and now he was sending a boy! Goliath roared with laughter. The sound was deafening, but David wasn't afraid.

The shepherd boy faced his enemy as Goliath came blundering forward.

"Come on," jeered Goliath. "I'm going to enjoy feeding you to the birds."

"You have come out to fight with a sword and a spear," said David boldly. "I have come in the name of God."

As Goliath moved towards him, David reached into his bag, took out a stone, and put it in his sling. He whirled it around so fast, you couldn't see it spinning. Then he took aim and let the stone fly.

He aim was good. The stone smashed into the middle of the giant's forehead. With a dreadful cry Goliath crashed to the ground and lay there, dead. The Philistines gasped.

Quick as a blink, David grabbed Goliath's sword and cut off the giant's head.

The Philistines were dumbfounded. Their champion fighter was dead. The shepherd boy had won the day. King Saul and his army cheered and cheered. They charged down the mountainside and chased the Philistines out of sight.

So David returned home a hero. He married the king's daughter, Princess Michal, and went to live in the palace.

And much, much later, when the old king died, David became king of Israel.

Daniel
in the Lions' Den

 King Darius was the king of Persia. He had more than a hundred officials to help him rule the land. His favourite was Daniel. Daniel was honest, wise, and loyal – and he never made mistakes. All the other men were jealous.

"King Darius never listens to us," they complained. "Daniel will be in charge of the country one day, you'll see."

It was true. King Darius had planned to make Daniel his most important official. Daniel's enemies wanted to get rid of him. But how? Daniel never did anything wrong. He wouldn't lose his job that way. They had to think of something else.

Now Daniel was a religious man. He worked hard for the king, but he was never too busy to pray to God. He prayed three times a day in his room in the palace. The other officials knew that and it gave them an idea.

One morning they went to see the king.

"We think there should be a new law," began one.

"To make your subjects obey you," said another.

They had written the law on a scroll for the king to sign. It said that people were forbidden to ask help from any god or man, except the king, for thirty days. If anyone disobeyed, they would be thrown to the lions! The king read it carefully.

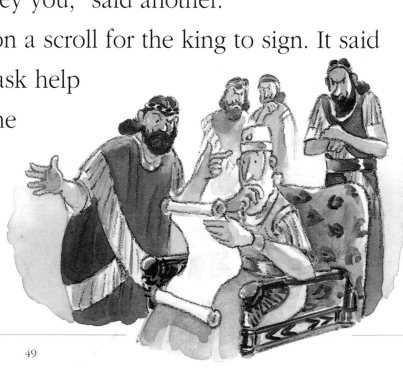

"So if you will just sign here," said one of the officials rather hurriedly, "we will see that everyone obeys it."

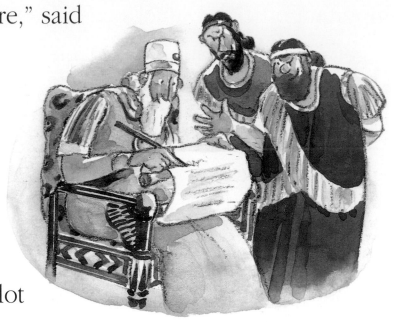

King Darius signed the new law. He didn't suspect a thing. How could he have guessed that it was a wicked plot to kill Daniel?

After Daniel found out that the law was signed, he went to his room to pray as usual and kneeled by his open window. His enemies spied on him as he prayed.

"Caught in the act!" they cried. And they marched right off to the king to tell him that Daniel prayed three times a day.

The king was very upset, but everyone, including Daniel, had to obey the law of the land. There was nothing King Darius could do to rescue him.

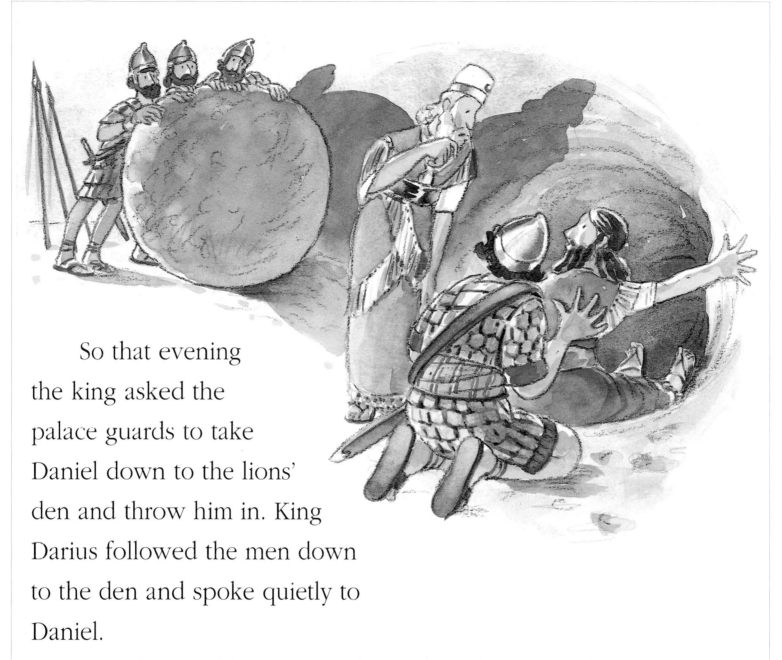

So that evening the king asked the palace guards to take Daniel down to the lions' den and throw him in. King Darius followed the men down to the den and spoke quietly to Daniel.

"I wish I could save you," he said. "Ask your god to protect you from the lions and keep you safe."

Then the guards pushed Daniel into the den and rolled a big stone across the entrance. The king walked sadly back to the palace. He was sure he would never see Daniel again.

Jonah made himself comfortable below deck and settled down for a nap. The sea was calm as they sailed out of the harbour. But soon a terrible storm blew up. The wind howled. Huge waves crashed over the sides of the boat.

"All hands on deck!" bellowed the captain. "Throw the cargo overboard."

That made the boat lighter and easier to steer. But the sailors were up to their knees in water. They were afraid and prayed to their gods. The captain went below to find Jonah, who was still asleep.

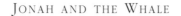

"Wake up!" shouted the captain. "We're in trouble. If the storm goes on like this, we'll all be drowned. Start praying to your god for help."

Jonah climbed on deck, where the crew was trying to find out who had caused the storm. They all wrote their names down and put them in a hat. The captain picked one out. It was Jonah's!

"Tell us! Who's to blame? And who are you anyway?" they cried.

Jonah had some explaining to do. He knew the storm was all his fault. He told the sailors that he worshipped God. God had seen him running away and was angry with him.

"Quick!" he said. "Throw me overboard. The storm will stop when I have gone."

The sailors were very scared and prayed that Jonah's God would understand. Then they threw Jonah out of the boat. And as soon as he splashed into the water, the wind dropped and the sea was as calm as a fish pond.

Down, down, down. Jonah sank like a stone. Seaweed wrapped itself around his neck and water bubbled in his mouth. It was dark and silent beneath the waves as Jonah sank deeper and deeper until . . . *Bump!* Jonah's head touched something slippery and soft.

He was about to grab it, when he found himself spinning around in a whirlpool. Jonah flapped his arms and spluttered. He was swept along a passageway, like a spider swirling down a plug hole. And just when it seemed he would never stop tumbling head over heels, he landed in a sort of cave.

He had been swallowed by a whale!

Jonah sat up and looked around. It was damp and sticky and smelled of rotting seaweed. Jonah cried. God would never find him now. He spent three long days and nights inside the whale. Then he thanked God for keeping him alive under the sea and asked for forgiveness. Jonah promised to go to Nineveh if he got out alive.

God knew Jonah was sorry. He forgave Jonah and told the whale to swim near a beach. Then the whale opened its enormous mouth, and spat Jonah out on to the sand. He was shaking with cold and hunger.

For a while Jonah lay in the sunshine and took deep breaths of fresh air. It was good to be out of that smelly whale. When Jonah had recovered, God spoke to him and told him to go to Nineveh.

"Tell the people to change their wicked ways or I will punish them," he said.

This time Jonah went to Nineveh at once. The people of that beautiful city listened to him. They were sorry for behaving so badly and began to change for the better.

God was very pleased. He forgave them for being so wicked and didn't punish them at all. Jonah was furious about it. He thought the people of Nineveh should have been punished.

"I knew this would happen!" he shouted. "I've come all this way for nothing."

God spoke quietly to Jonah. "Don't be angry," he said. "I forgave them because they were sorry."

Jonah thought for a moment and said, "Just as you forgave me inside the whale?"

"Yes," said God. "It's best to forgive."

And Jonah had to agree he was right.

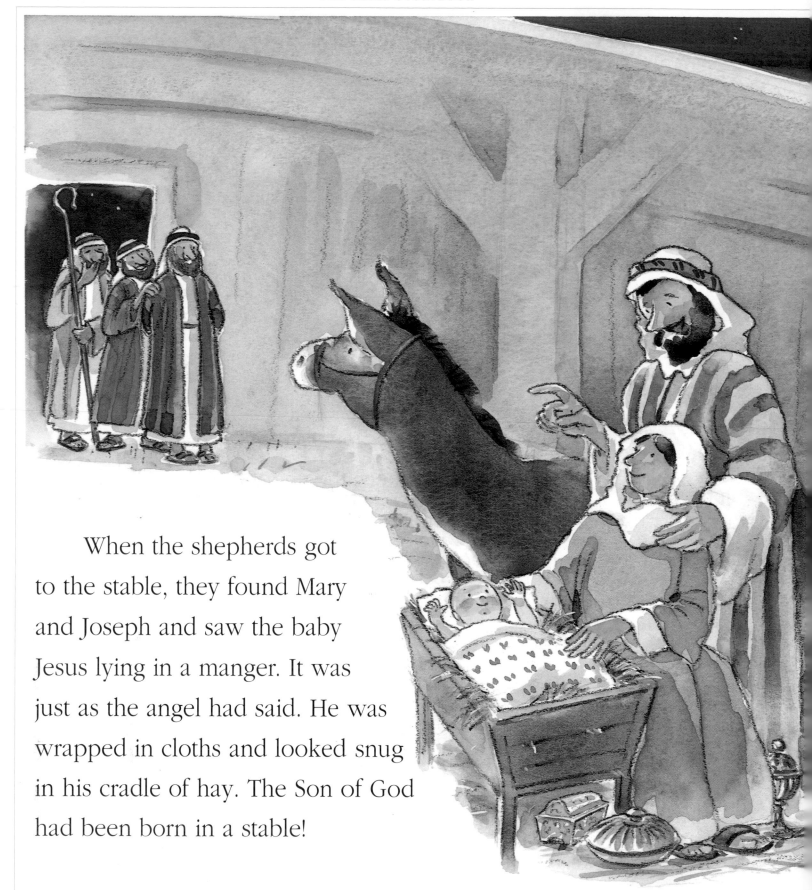

When the shepherds got to the stable, they found Mary and Joseph and saw the baby Jesus lying in a manger. It was just as the angel had said. He was wrapped in cloths and looked snug in his cradle of hay. The Son of God had been born in a stable!

The shepherds were not the only ones to hear about the baby. Three wise men, living far away in another country, had been told about the new king too. They travelled all the way to Bethlehem on camels, following a big, bright star. The star took them right to the place where Jesus lay.

Mary and Joseph welcomed the travellers as they came to worship the royal child. The wise men brought the baby precious gifts of gold, frankincense, and myrrh – gifts fit for a king – that very first Christmas, nearly two thousand years ago.

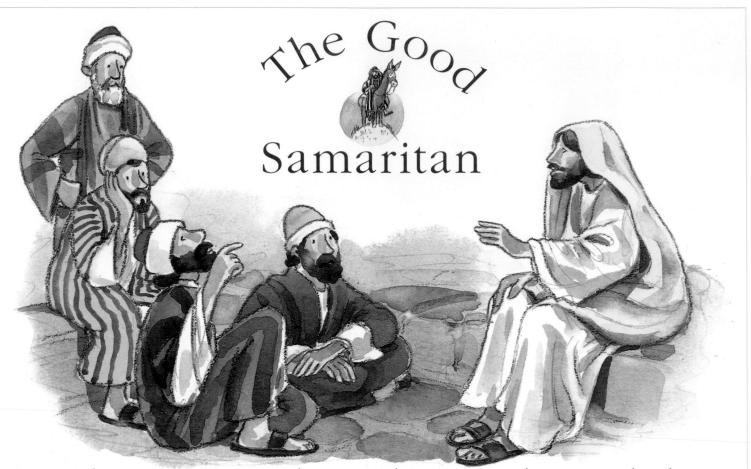

The Good Samaritan

When Jesus grew up, he spent his time teaching people about God and being kind to one another. He was always being asked questions. Sometimes Jesus answered with a story, and asked his listeners to work out the answer for themselves. Which is how this story came about.

A clever teacher of the law once said to Jesus, "What do I have to do to live forever? The law says we should love God with all our hearts and love our neighbours as much as ourselves. But who is my neighbour?" The teacher was testing Jesus. He hoped to hear that he should love only his friends. So Jesus told him a story about a traveller.

A man was walking from Jerusalem to Jericho. It was a long walk and the road passed through lonely, hilly country. It was a dangerous road. Robbers and bandits hid among the rocks.

Sure enough, as the traveller walked along, a gang of robbers sprang from a hiding place. They knocked the man to the ground, beat him, and stole his money and clothes. Then the gang ran off, leaving him lying in the road.

After a while a priest came along. The very person to help someone in trouble, you might think. But he didn't. He took one look at the injured man and hurried by on the other side of the road. He was afraid the robbers might attack him too.

Shortly afterwards another man came along. He worked in the temple. But he didn't stop either. He took a closer look at the man, then like the priest, hurried by on the other side.

The sun beat down and the flies buzzed around the man's wounds. It seemed as if the poor traveller was to be left to die on that desolate country road.

Much later the sound of donkey's hooves could be heard in the distance. It was a man on his way to Jericho. He was a Samaritan.

Now, the man who had been injured was a Jew, and the Jews and the Samaritans were old enemies. The Jews thought of the Samaritans as foreigners and wouldn't speak to them. So it was unlikely the Samaritan would stop to help.

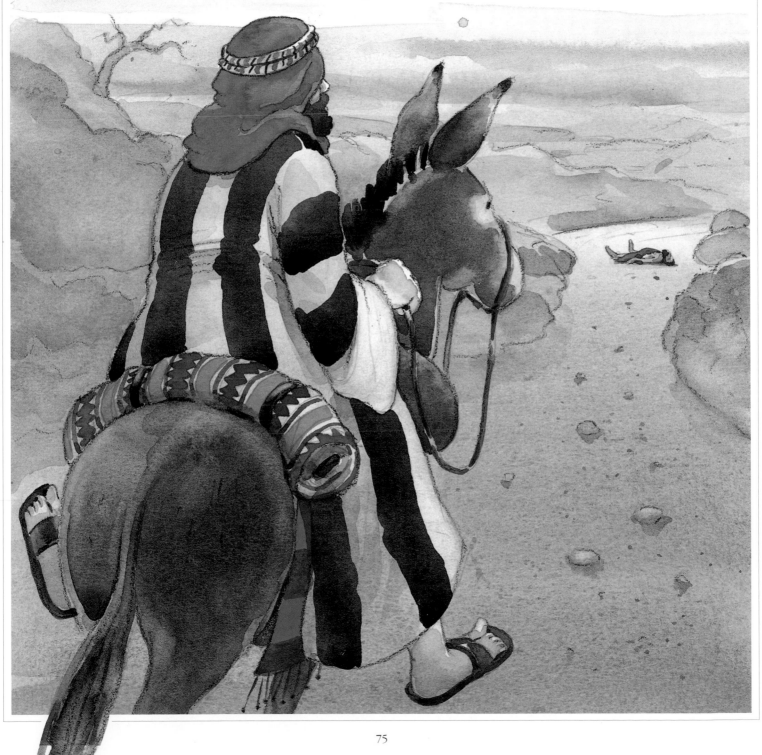

But as soon as the Samaritan saw the injured man, he got off his donkey and went to him. He took wine from his saddlebag and cleaned the man's wounds. Then he bathed the wounds with soothing oil and bandaged them. After that the Samaritan gently lifted the man on to his donkey and took him to the nearest inn.

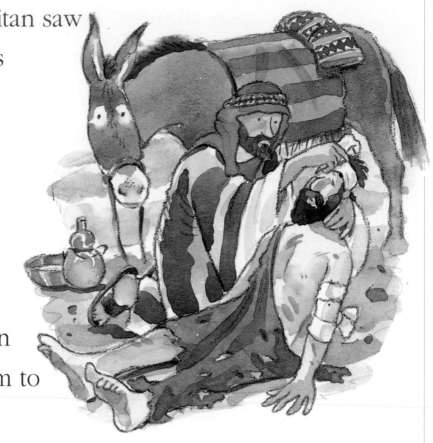

He stayed with the man that night to make sure he was comfortable.

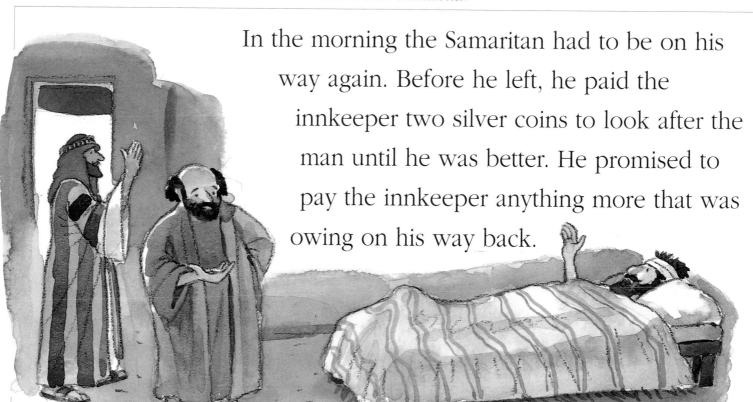

In the morning the Samaritan had to be on his way again. Before he left, he paid the innkeeper two silver coins to look after the man until he was better. He promised to pay the innkeeper anything more that was owing on his way back.

When Jesus had finished telling this story, he turned to the clever teacher and said, "Which of the three men do you think loved the injured man like a neighbour?"

The clever teacher didn't feel quite so clever now.

"The Samaritan," he admitted. "The one who was kind to him."

"You're right," said Jesus. "Now go, and be like him."

So that was it! In all the hustle and bustle, at the very moment the woman had touched his cloak, Jesus had felt some healing power flow out of him.

Jesus looked at the woman with such kindness. "Your trust in me has cured you," he said gently.

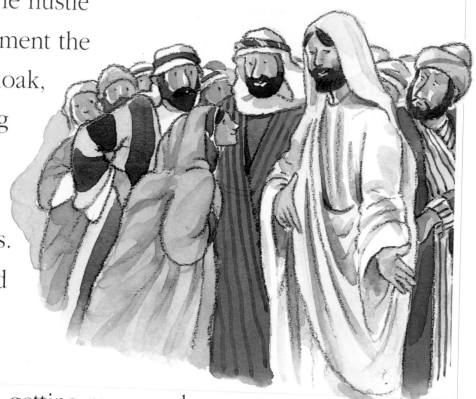

Meanwhile Jairus had been getting more and more anxious. Every second counted if Jesus was to make his daughter well. Yet here he was, stopping to heal this woman as if he had all the time in the world!

Jairus was about to plead with Jesus to hurry up, when he saw his servant coming to meet him. He had sad news.

"Your daughter is dead," he said. "There is no need to trouble Jesus anymore."

Jairus wept. His daughter had just died, and the only man who could have saved her was so near. But Jesus simply turned to Jairus and said, "Go on trusting me."

Then he took three of his friends, Peter, James and John, and went to see the child. Jairus and his wife cried as Jesus sat down at her bedside.

Jesus took the small, cold hand in his. "Get up, my child," he said quietly.

The little girl's eyes flickered open. As she felt her strength returning, she sat up, smiled at Jesus . . . and jumped out of bed!

You can imagine how thankful those parents were to see their daughter alive and well again.

Jesus smiled at them. He loved children and it made him happy too.

"And now," he said, "it's time to prepare some food. I think you'll find your daughter is hungry!"

The Story of the Loaves and Fishes

No one knows the name of the little boy in this story, so I shall call him Thomas.

Thomas lived in a tiny village tucked away in the hills overlooking Lake Galilee. It was a lonely life and he was often bored. He had no brothers or sisters to play with that I know of – only a few goats. And they weren't much fun.

One day Thomas decided to go for a walk down by the lake. He liked climbing rocks and looking for crabs in the sand.

"Take some food," said his mother, "and be careful."

She packed a bag with five barley loaves and two small fishes, and Thomas set off. He was scrambling down a bank when he heard the sound of voices.

Thomas looked, and to his surprise, he saw a great many people walking along the shore. They were coming towards him. Usually he would be lucky to find one person to talk to. But today there were hundreds! Thomas ran over to a group of children. They pointed to a boat on the lake.

"Look! Jesus is coming," explained a little girl, waving to the boat. "Let's go and meet him."

Thomas looked down on the lake and saw a boat full of men approaching. Jesus was sitting in the middle.

Jesus also saw the crowd coming and had pity on them. They had followed him all this way and had brought nothing with them to eat.

"Where can we buy enough food to feed all these people?" Jesus asked his friend Philip. He already knew the answer, but Philip didn't know that.

"It would cost a fortune," replied Philip. "Two hundred silver coins wouldn't buy enough bread for each to have even a little piece."

Andrew, another friend of Jesus, had seen Thomas with his lunch.

"Look," said Andrew, "that boy has some food."

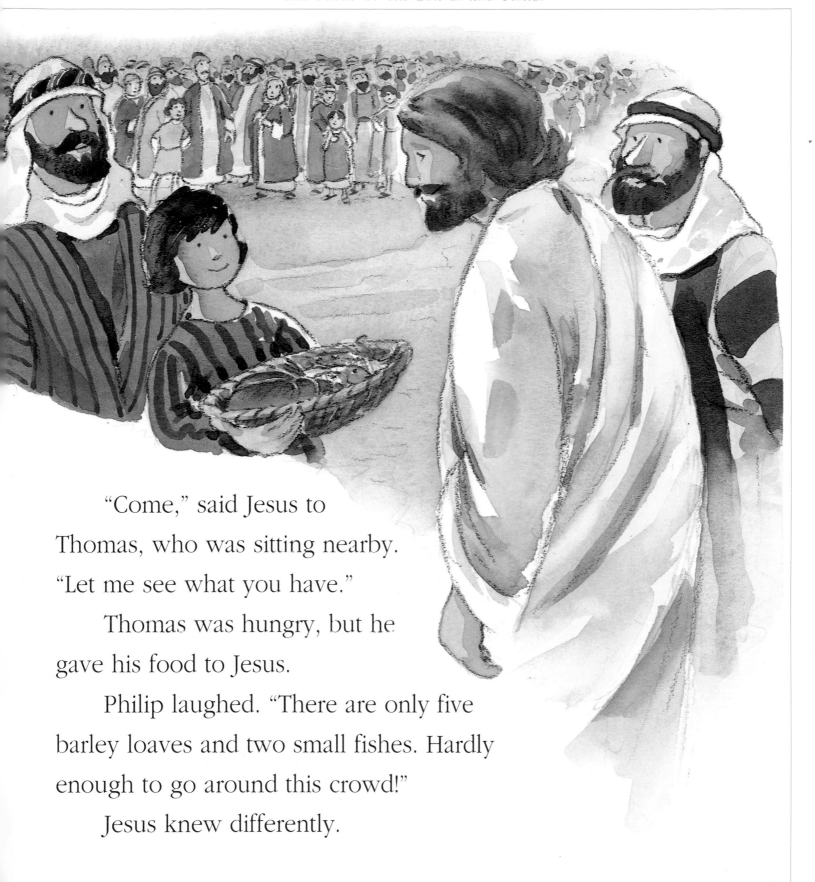

"Come," said Jesus to
Thomas, who was sitting nearby.
"Let me see what you have."

Thomas was hungry, but he
gave his food to Jesus.

Philip laughed. "There are only five
barley loaves and two small fishes. Hardly
enough to go around this crowd!"

Jesus knew differently.

"Tell the people to sit down," he told Philip and Andrew as he took the food. While they were seating the crowd in small groups, Jesus gave thanks to God and began to break the food into small pieces.

As Jesus broke the bread and fish, he gave out handfuls to share with everyone there. Handfuls and handfuls! Enough to feed all those people until they were full. Thomas was astonished. Jesus had fed over five thousand people from his five barley loaves and two small fishes.

At the end of the meal Jesus told his friends to pick up any food that was left over. He didn't want to waste anything. And do you know, they collected twelve baskets full of scraps!

That evening Thomas ran home to tell his mother all that had happened. It was a day he would remember for the rest of his life.